Jesus is Clothed with the Cross: A Child's Reflection on the Stations of the Cross

MATTHEW B. P. WONG

Text Copyright © 2013 Matthew B. P. Wong, Illustrations © 2013 Mary J. C. Wong

All rights reserved.

ISBN:1490949178
ISBN-13: 978-1490949178

DEDICATION

I dedicate these written words to my God.

CONTENTS

	Acknowledgments	i
Station 1	Jesus is Condemned to Death	Pg. 2
Station 2	Jesus Bears His Cross	Pg. 4
Station 3	Jesus Falls the First Time	Pg. 6
Station 4	Jesus Meets His Mother	Pg. 8
Station 5	Jesus is Helped by Simon	Pg. 10
Station 6	Jesus and Veronica	Pg. 12
Station 7	Jesus Falls the Second Time	Pg. 14
Station 8	Jesus Speaks to the Women	Pg. 16
Station 9	Jesus Falls the Third Time	Pg. 18
Station 10	Jesus is Stripped of His Garments	Pg. 20
Station 11	Jesus is Nailed to the Cross	Pg. 22
Station 12	Jesus Dies on the Cross	Pg. 24
Station 13	Jesus is Taken Down from the Cross	Pg. 26
Station 14	Jesus is Laid in the Sepulchre	Pg. 28
	Prayer after Stations	Pg. 30

ACKNOWLEDGMENTS

Many thanks to my Mom and Dad for teaching me about Christ. I also thank my sister for illustrating this book.

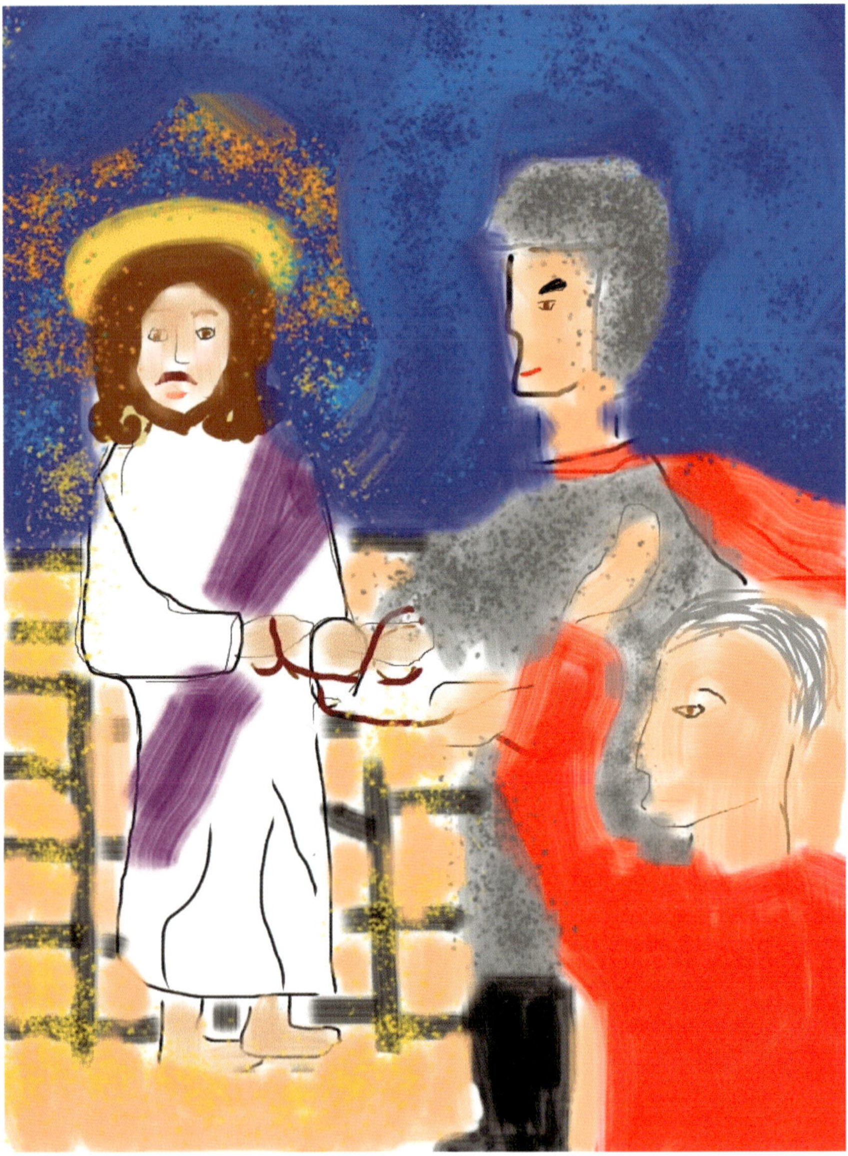

FIRST STATION - JESUS IS CONDEMNED TO DEATH

Jesus our humble Savior is condemned to death. If I were Jesus, I would be terrified. Even though Jesus struggles with this thought, He bears it. This teaches us that we should not fear death. It reminds us that before our time comes, we should pray and begin a personal relationship with God in order to explore the wonders of Heaven with Him.

Prayer

Lord, please help me be faithful and not fear death. Guide me to Your Light so I may return to my real home when my time comes. Amen.

JESUS IS CLOTHED WITH THE CROSS

SECOND STATION - JESUS BEARS HIS CROSS

Jesus must be nailed to a cross in order to save us from our sins. But first He has to carry His heavy cross to the Place of the Skull. As Jesus bears His cross, we also need to carry our own spiritual crosses. This means that we have to bear our sufferings peacefully.

Prayer

Lord, lift us up when we fall, help us bear the burdens that we can hardly carry and bring us to victory. Amen.

JESUS IS CLOTHED WITH THE CROSS

THIRD STATION - JESUS FALLS THE FIRST TIME

Under the weight of the cross, Jesus suddenly falls. But He immediately rises back up. If we fall, we should focus on God but ignore the "bad wolf" who tempts us to give up. Let us ask God to give us an easier journey to Heaven.

Prayer

Lord, help us on this difficult path while carrying our crosses to Heaven. Help those who are not on the path to Heaven and guide them back through the Holy Spirit. Like You, help us rise quickly after we fall. Amen.

JESUS IS CLOTHED WITH THE CROSS

FOURTH STATION - JESUS MEETS HIS MOTHER

Mary, Jesus' mother must be frightened to see her Son in pain. However, Jesus faithfully carries on in order to fulfill His Father's will. When Mary sees Him, she embraces Him. Mary loves Him and she loves us because she is the mother of Jesus who Loves us. And we can always run to our mothers for help. This means we should honor Mary and seek her protection.

Prayer

Lord and Mary, please help me to be strong when I am at my weakest. Please remind me that You are always with me and I am never alone. Amen.

JESUS IS CLOTHED WITH THE CROSS

FIFTH STATION - JESUS IS HELPED BY SIMON

A man named Simon helps Jesus carry his cross. This teaches us that we should always help our neighbor when they are in need. As Simon helps Jesus bear His cross, we should help bear our neighbors' crosses. Helping our neighbor is like helping God.

Prayer

God, please teach us how to care for each other as though we were caring for You. Please, watch over us and help us to watch out for each other. Amen.

JESUS IS CLOTHED WITH THE CROSS

SIXTH STATION - JESUS AND VERONICA

As Veronica cleans the Lord's face, we are reminded that God cleans us to. He purifies us by forgiving our sins when we go to confession. When He takes away our sins, we become as innocent as lambs and as pure as infants. It is like beginning a new life for us.

Prayer

Lord, please clean our soul and purify us. Clean us and guide our lives back on to the path to Heaven. Amen.

JESUS IS CLOTHED WITH THE CROSS

SEVENTH STATION - JESUS FALLS THE SECOND TIME

As Jesus continues His path to the Place of the Skull, He falls again because of the weight of His cross. That means that we are not perfect and that we will stumble many times. However, we must continue the journey to Heaven despite stumbling.

Prayer

Lord, as I fall, help me to recover. After helping me get up, keep me close to You so I can always run back to You when I need Your assistance. Amen.

JESUS IS CLOTHED WITH THE CROSS

EIGHTH STATION - JESUS SPEAKS TO THE WOMEN

When Jesus speaks to the women, He tells them to weep for their sins, but not to weep for Him. We too should repent for our sins and earnestly feel sorry for them. Do not be timid about asking Him for forgiveness because God will not only forgive us, but also forget all of our sins.

Prayer

Lord help us to confidently come to You to ask for forgiveness. Amen.

JESUS IS CLOTHED WITH THE CROSS

NINTH STATION - JESUS FALLS THE THIRD TIME

When Jesus finally reaches the Place of the Skull, He falls down for the third time. When we fall while trying to fulfill God's Will, we should ask Him for help and comfort. Even though we fall, that does not mean that we have failed God. Look at Jesus. He always follows His Father's Will. We too should let go of our own will and follow God's.

Prayer

Lord, hear us when we are desperate for your help. Help us see that You have a better plan for us. Amen.

JESUS IS CLOTHED WITH THE CROSS

TENTH STATION - JESUS IS STRIPPED OF HIS GARMENTS

Jesus is stripped of His garments when He arrives at the Place of the Skull. This represents that we should not be so attached to earthly things. Instead, we should focus on going to Heaven to share eternal life with God. We should trade our earthly things for heavenly treasures.

Prayer

Lord, help us let go of earthly things and remind us of how great Heaven is. Amen.

JESUS IS CLOTHED WITH THE CROSS

ELEVENTH STATION - JESUS IS NAILED TO THE CROSS

How terrifying it must have been to see our Savior being nailed to a cross! This means that we as His followers are also nailed to our crosses when we obey the Commandments. However, our pain on our crosses is no match for Jesus' suffering on His cross. There is no way to make it up to Him because He is God suffering and He obtains for us this free gift of the Father's forgiveness.

Prayer

Lord, please help me follow your commandments that You gave Moses on Mount Sinai. Amen.

JESUS IS CLOTHED WITH THE CROSS

TWELFTH STATION - JESUS DIES ON THE CROSS

When Jesus dies on the cross, the sky becomes dark, even though it is only three o'clock in the afternoon. There is a great earthquake. All of the Earth weeps after His death. Many of Jesus' disciples are also weeping. But despite the mourning, we should be thankful. He dies for our sins and opens the gates to Heaven. We now have the royal blood of God because of what Jesus accomplishes for us. If we choose to follow Him, we will go to Heaven with God.

Prayer

Lord, thank you for opening the door to Heaven for us by dying on the cross! Help me reach Heaven so I can share eternal happiness and love with You. Amen.

JESUS IS CLOTHED WITH THE CROSS

THIRTEENTH STATION - JESUS IS TAKEN DOWN FROM THE CROSS

After Jesus dies, Jesus is taken down from His cross. Mary holds His lifeless body close in her arms weeping. When it is our turn to go Heaven, the Holy Family will also come to take us down from our crosses.

Prayer

Lord, help me go straight to Heaven when my time comes and hold me close as You carry me home. Amen.

JESUS IS CLOTHED WITH THE CROSS

FOURTEENTH STATION - JESUS IS LAID IN THE SEPULCHRE

Those who help take Jesus down from His cross lay Him down in a Sepulchre. They mourn His death while the people who persecute Jesus are triumphant. But Jesus is not actually gone because He returns to God the Father with all the souls whom He has saved and He is present with us right now. So in reality, Jesus is the triumphant one.

Prayer

O Lord, thank you for saving us from our sins. Let me one day triumphantly return to Paradise like You. Amen.

JESUS IS CLOTHED WITH THE CROSS

PRAYER AFTER STATIONS

Jesus, You became an example of humility, obedience, and patience, proceeded me on the way of life bearing Your cross. Grant that, inflamed by Your love, I may cheerfully take upon myself the sweet yoke of Your Gospel together with mortification of the cross and follow You as a true disciple so that I may be united with You in Heaven. Amen.

ABOUT THE AUTHOR AND ILLUSTRATOR

    Matthew and Mary are ten-year old twins attending Fifth grade in California. They both enjoy basketball, reading, and doing mathematics. Matthew likes to express himself through music, especially the violin. Mary likes to express herself through visual art. They also like to attend daily mass with their parents whenever possible.

Printed in Great Britain
by Amazon.co.uk, Ltd.,
Marston Gate.